WRITE TO HEAL

TOM BIRD

SOJOURN PUBLISHING, LLC
SEDONA, AZ

Write To Heal

Copyright © 2013 by Tom Bird

For permissions:

Sojourn Publishing, LLC, 280 Foothills South Dr.,
Sedona, AZ 86336

ISBN-13: 978-1-62747-005-6 (paperback)
ISBN-13: 978-1-62747-006-3 (ebook)

Printed in the United States of America

CONTENTS

Introduction

WRITING, ESPECIALLY OF A BOOK, HAS BEEN known as a great healer for centuries. In fact, it was the great Aristotle who said that to live a full and complete life one of the three things every human being needed to do was to write a book.

Our awareness of these special kinds of healings provided by writing—especially of a book—has been furthered substantially through the work of many. In fact, works on the healing aspects of writing have mysteriously paralleled the growth of strife and tension in the average life. Nothing ever happens without a reason, including, I imagine, this parallel climb as well.

In just the last few decades, Gabriele Rico (*Writing the Natural Way*, Tarcher Books, 1983) illustrated for us how to harness the creative/healing abilities that resulted from the work of Nobel Prize winner Roger Sperry, creator of the Right/Left Brain Theory, as well as from Julia Cameron through her book *The Artist's Way* (Tarcher Books, 1992). Many others also contributed to getting us writing every day. Authors such as Lucia Capacchione and her book *The Power of Your Other Hand* (Newcastle, 1988) and Rico, who followed up her first book with *Pain and Possibility: Writing Your Way through Personal Crisis* (Tarcher Books, 1991), helped us better harness the healing powers of writing for our own personal and professional benefits.

The healing concept of writing has also been depicted in real-to-life movies such as *Finding Forrester* and *Dead Poets Society*.

Lastly, the healing power of writing, and how certain individuals may have been soulfully drawn into situations that caused them to access it, can be seen in hundreds of contemporary books. *Angela's Ashes* (Scribner, 1996), is the best selling work of Frank McCourt, who healed himself from the effects of an Irish Catholic, alcoholic, and severely abusive upbringing through the writing of his classic work. Rubin "Hurricane" Carter found healing through the writing of his best seller, *Eye of the Hurricane: My Path from Darkness to Freedom* (Chicago Review Press, 2011), which he penned with nothing else to do while unjustly locked away in prison on trumped-up murder charges. Solzhenitsyn did his best writing while locked away in a Siberian prison as well.

What makes this book different from the others

mentioned? Simple. *Write to Heal* builds upon the works of these great pioneers and then goes way beyond anything else being offered on this topic. It goes to the core, the soul of us all both as writers and as human beings. It then leads you, the only person who is capable of doing this, to remove any and all blockages that could in any way keep you from living to your potential as both a person and/or as an author.

Sounds like a tall order, I know. However, the healing power of writing has surely been thoroughly illustrated over the years. So much so that I feel this book comprises the first and most essential step any would-be author needs to take to clear out his/her clogged, creative passageway so that there is enough room for a book to be birthed.

This book will work equally well for proven authors and average human beings with a deep desire to contribute to the betterment of life. Through their use of this book, both will be freed to create and heartfeltly express what they have to share, whether it be in the form of a book or something else, with as little strife and as much joy, happiness, laughter, and speed as possible.

"Why writing?" you ask.

I am not sure that I can answer that question to your level of satisfaction.

All I can say is that through my work with more than 80,000 would-be authors over the last thirty years, I have seen lives, relationships, deep and sometimes forgotten wounds healed, almost instantaneously, through the designs captured and set forth in this book.

If pressed for an answer, I would have to say that when writing with the methods outlined in all the books on writing, including this one, something beautiful and unique transpires. The writer becomes as one, at least I believe, connecting directly with the Ultimate Force, who I prefer to refer to as God.

As this returning home of sorts transpires, the essence of that Force that we embody directly connects with That From Which We Were Born, creating a perfect union. When that happens, and as that Force comes pouring through us, we cannot help but to be healed by this perfect union, what we were meant to deliver onto Earth. As a result, everything around us heals as well.

We all owe the results of this amazing transition to writing, which is why so many of us are drawn directly to this art form to pen our books, allowing us to heal and release our divine, expressionistic potential as well. For then and only then, after a transition such as this happens, can we do one of the most important things we were born onto the planet to do, which is to deliver the message, no matter what form it takes, that we were born to leave behind.

This book is the first step in creating that divinely personal ability for you.

Tom Bird

CHAPTER ONE

HOW WRITING ACTUALLY CREATES WHOLE BODY HEALING AND THUS CHANGE

To BEGIN ON THE MOST EXCITING OF ALL JOURNEYS that this book offers, it is first of all important to understand why and how we strayed off the divine path we now seek and got so mucked up.

In doing so, I am simply going to cut to the chase and get right to the point. That way you can move through all of this necessary material as quickly as possible and get back to where it is you long to return as quickly as possible.

Simply put, there are four aspects to every being: the physical, mental, emotional, and spiritual.

Each is comprised of the same exact energy, but what differentiates between them is the denseness that each of the four aspects take on.

The physical is easily the densest, followed by the mental, the emotional, and then the spiritual.

The Ultimate Spirit or Force, who is trying to connect with us and from whom we were all spawned, is even lighter and less dense than the spirit within each of us. To directly connect with The Ultimate Spirit/Force, which is our divine birthright, we must raise our vibrational level above that of the mental, physical, and emotional sides of ourselves. We can do so in a measurable way, which is not available in such a manner in any other art form, through our writing when we write at 1,500 words an hour and above.

In fact, you may have already innocently experienced this unique connection with your own communion using the art form of writing, when your pen just seemed to be flying across the page or your fingers moved like lightning as they jumped across your keyboard.

Yet, even during what could be viewed as a very frantic time, you were calm and at peace. You may have even lost track of time as aspects of this Ultimate Force, such as wisdom, guidance, or understanding, came pouring into the slower, flowing aspects of yourself.

If you have experienced anything like this in the past, you have felt the healing power that comes with the connection of writing.

You probably just didn't know what you were experiencing and if you did, you didn't know how to recreate it. Or you innocently didn't stay with it long enough to feel its full permanent effects.

But when The Ultimate Force, through which we have all been born, comes through you via your writing at this speed and you stay with it long enough, all aspects of you are soon healed: the mental, physical, emotional, and your often ignored or unappreciated spiritual side as well.

Chapter Two

What You Need to Consistently Reach That Speed

To reach or exceed the writing speed to which I am referring is simple and easy.

In fact, over 95 percent of those who have entered my classes, lectures, and retreats for the last three decades are easily able to reach that speed within a few minutes of instruction and guidance.

That's all.

So how can you do it? Simple.

Go to my website, *www.TomBird.com*.

On my homepage you will see a tab entitled "Freebies." Click on that tab and download the free copy of my CD, *Transitioning Back to the Author You Were Meant To Be*.

Don't allow yourself to become intimidated by

the title of the CD. I am not trying to make you into an author you may not be. However, your use of the relaxation exercise that comprises Track One of the CD will relax your physical, mental, and emotional aspects to such an extent that your spiritual side will then be able to reach up and directly connect with the Spirit.

Go to my site and download this CD right now; you will need it to set the stage from where you will write, and thus, where you will connect through your writing.

CHAPTER THREE

TIME AND SPACE

NEITHER THIS SHORT BUT POWERFUL BOOK, NOR anything else, will be able to help you overcome your past, heal, and step into your true purpose, unless you create space and time for it to do so.

I know, I know, you may feel that you don't have enough time. Most people who are consciously or subconsciously suffering the most oftentimes use 'a lack of time' as their greatest excuse for not facing that which they need to face yet are afraid to face the most.

Fortunately, as the result of the directness and efficiency of this system, you really won't need much time, but you will need space and alone time so you can devote yourself to allowing the power that comes through writing to move through you.

When is the best time to find that space and time?

Early in the morning, middle of the night, or after just awakening from a good night's sleep or a good nap. This is when the three aspects, other than the spiritual, are not awake yet and thus easier to move through.

Keeping this fact in mind when approaching the following exercises will help you get the most out of them.

CHAPTER FOUR

CONSISTENCY

A S YOU WILL NOTICE FROM THE COPY OF MY CD YOU should have downloaded by now, there are two tracks.

Track One is composed of a relaxation exercise; the authors with whom I have had the pleasure to work refer to it as The Author Within State. That is the place where the Spirit Within You connects with the Spirit or Force Who Created You.

The Second Track of the CD is designed to keep you in that stage once you get there, so the communication of your soul with this Force continues long enough to breed permanent changes.

It accomplishes this task through the combination of rhythmless and relaxing background music along with subliminal commands.

Subliminal commands are words recorded at such a low decibel level that they are unable to be heard by your conscious mind, or left brain, but they can still be heard by your right brain, or creative/expressive side through which your Author Within speaks and The Ultimate Forces comes through.

Try not to let the presence of the subliminal commands on this CD concern you. Don't use that as your excuse not to heal, for there is no reason to. In fact, here are a few of the commands on the CD. As you can see they are non-invasive.

- You are safe, you are appreciated, you are loved.
- The world is awaiting the birth of this very special part of you.
- Releasing is easy. All it translates to is letting go.

Breathe out any disruptive emotions that are trying to release themselves now. Breathe. You don't have to understand them, embrace them, mourn them, or forgive yourself for them; just let them go. Let them go now. Breathe. Breathe and live...now.

When using this CD, always play Track One first to get you into the Author Within State and then let the CD roll over onto Track Two to keep you in that state.

Restart or reset Track Two if your writing session goes longer than the hour it is programmed to run to insure that you remain in your Author Within State.

CHAPTER FIVE

QUESTIONS

EVEN THOUGH IT MAY BE OF GREAT SIGNIFICANCE, AT the most basic of all levels, having a talk with our parental Ultimate Force is just like any other conversation; meaning one party talks and the other one listens.

That also means that if you ask a question of this Force, a reply will be forthcoming.

So it is okay, in fact necessary, for you to ask questions of The Ultimate Force to be able to get the replies that you seek.

To do so effectively though, you have to remain quiet to hear, feel, or see (depending upon which way you choose to receive the reply) the answer.

What that equates to is remaining in The Author Within State, which the CD will do for you, by keeping quiet (especially) your jealous mind, so it doesn't try to squeeze you out of your conscious connection with The Ultimate Force.

Chapter Six

Your First Exercises

THE FOLLOWING EXERCISES WERE CHOSEN FOR THEIR healing abilities and because they were the most effective in my work with aspiring authors over the last thirty years.

Before you begin, it is highly suggested that you properly prepare yourself to write.

Meaning, besides having your CD set up to play, you should have several pens sitting close by as well as a lineless pad of paper.

In regard to writing longhand, since typing is a left-brained drill, doing so simply, at least initially, creates the best opportunity possible for you to get into and remain in connection with The Ultimate Force (TUF).

Regarding the pens, make sure they are gel or ball points because they will flow the best across the paper, making it easiest for you to keep up with the speed of TUF's spirit as it flows through you.

Lineless paper is free of rules and regulations, unconditional in nature, just the way the spirit of TUF likes it, which also affords you the finest results as well.

Since what you give to a situation is oftentimes mirrored by what you get out of it, it is strongly suggested that you allow yourself to go deeply into the following exercises, being very thorough and trying to avoid rushing to finish them.

However, even when you approach each one of these with great depth, each one will have its own personality. Thus, some will write themselves out quickly while others will take several writing sessions spread potentially over days to finish.

Just keep in mind when doing these exercises, which are designed to spark a full-blown physical/mental/emotional/spiritual healing in you, that each one will seem to have its own path, voice, direction and purpose, and remember to allow yourself to follow each response wherever it goes.

That will also prove to be especially true with the "why?" portion of the next three exercises, which, by their very nature, will be asking the spirit of TUF to delve most deeply into the deepest confines of a reply.

Also keep in mind that the questions and statements that follow in the exercises may lead to TUF providing you with further questions and answers that It seeks to address for you, and is just waiting for you to pose.

So, feel free at any time to share whatever it is you

re being called to ask. For it is probably the
UF coming through you prompting you to
tion that it wants to address.

TUF doesn't ask Itself that sort of question, for to do so would be in violation of your divine free will. Yet, encouraging you to ask a question of Itself is acceptable.

In addition, make sure you always use the CD you downloaded from my site to get you into your Author Within State before doing any of the following exercises. Trying to pursue them without doing so would be like emotional suicide because the chance that your consciousness would be clear enough on its own to reach the speed necessary to connect directly with The Source is very slim.

Lastly, the length of time it will take you to follow the exercises is clearly between you and TUF.

Some of you may move through them all in one session, some several, some within a few hours. Others may take days, weeks, or a month. Others may go through the following exercises several times, making more than one lap.

In this one area of your life, just let TUF lead you to see what will happen. If you are anything like those who have gone through this before, you will quite possibly be amazed.

Here's the first exercise.

After taking time to get into your Author Within State via my CD, ask of The Spirit:

If I were a road, where would I lead and why?

CHAPTER SEVEN

NUMBER TWO

AFTER YOU HAVE FINISHED WITH YOUR REPLY TO THE first exercise and any side questions that may have surfaced and needed to be addressed as well, make sure you are in your Author Within State and ask the following of yourself and TUF.

If I were a fish, animal or fowl, what would I be, and why?

Chapter Eight

Now Try This One

What one situation or event, more than any other in my life, has done more to make me who I am; and why and how has it done so?

CHAPTER NINE

WHO, WHAT, WHEN, HOW?

Who has wronged you, hurt you?
What was it that was done?
When did it transpire and how has that
adversely affected you in the direction and
the quality of your life?

TIME TO GET THOSE QUESTIONS ANSWERED, TO LAY IT all out.

Make sure that your pens, paper, snacks, and water are handy, that you are alone and will remain unbothered (having some tissues nearby wouldn't be a bad idea either), then turn on the first track of the CD I asked you to download. Follow the instructions on it. Allow it to roll onto the second track and as it does, begin to respond to the previous questions on your lineless paper. Be very thorough, even if it means coming back to this exercise for multiple sessions. Leave no one or no thing behind. Release it all. Begin doing so now, right now.

Chapter Ten

The Next One

1. Turn on the first track of the CD you downloaded from my website and follow the instructions through the relaxation exercise.

2. Once the CD begins to roll onto the second track, on a piece of lineless paper, one at a time, write down the name of the first person or the description of the first situation that needs to be forgiven. Whether you feel that he/she/it deserves to be forgiven does not matter. This is not a subjective decision you are making; it is a definitive action that you are taking. Write down that name and then next to it write down the words, "name or situation I forgive you for." Then write down whatever it is that you forgive

this person or situation for.

3. Especially in the initial stages of this exercise it may not come easy and you may feel a significant amount of anger and resistance. If that happens, that is good, for it will verify that your energy is moving, that your internal resistance and pain are being shaken and calling to be released. If this happens, let it out. Allow yourself to have a primal scream, cry, yell, cuss, beat a pillow, write it all out, whatever you have to do to facilitate it leaving you. For behind that resistance and pain is the ability to forgive and then behind the forgiveness is the enlightenment and peace we all seek; which comprises our most natural of all states.

4. Stay with the first name you chose to forgive. Flush out your pain and resistance for as long as you need, even if it takes several sessions over days or weeks. Stay with this process on the first name you chose until you can write down the words from #2 above, forgive this person or situation and feel nothing. Then, and only then, will it be the forgiveness you seek.

5. As you can imagine, this exercise may take a significant amount of time to move through name-by-name-by-name. You will see that as you move down your list, moving through each

name will become progressively easier and faster. That is because in some unique way all of these pains and unresolved issues, which are dying to be forgiven and released, are all tied together. So to remove one is somehow part of removing all. Stay with it, nonetheless, and don't move onto the next chapter until you have fully completed this exercise. For to move ahead without doing so would be like going on a major shopping spree only to arrive home and find your closets are already completely stocked with clothes—ones you no longer want, and thus there is no room for those you just bought and which you really want.

Chapter Eleven

Man or Woman in the Mirror

As I am sure you have become aware by now, it is not enough to forgive others. The enlightenment we seek, which is available through our writing, and which will lead us to the peace we all innately desire, is only totally available through complete forgiveness, including of ourselves.

That's where this chapter comes in.

How could that be?

Each person and situation that you worked with and through in the previous chapter was an angel in disguise reflecting back, or responsible for, manifesting a certain lesson you need to resolve and dissolve in your karma (unresolved "stuff") allowing you to step into your dharma (life purpose).

Remember Christ's forty days and forty nights in the desert? Get what I am talking about now?

What we have been doing together over the last few chapters comprises that for you as well.

Like Christ, you are tearing off the band-aid quickly as opposed to allowing life to do it for you at the more frightening speed of one hair at a time.

Christ did not come into His full enlightenment, nor Buddha nor Muhammad either, until they went through their tests of time.

This is your test of time, your chance to step fully into your enlightenment and fully live for yourself and all those you love around you.

Man/Woman in the Mirror

1. Turn on the CD and move through the first track.

2. Once the second track begins, start writing on a large lineless piece of paper all the things you feel you need to forgive yourself for, many of which will be tied directly to what you had to forgive others for and everything else you had to forgive from the previous chapter.

3. This is not a place to allow yourself to run dry. Take on the responsibility of completing this exercise, for if you don't, all that follows will

not work for you to its maximum potential. As a result, you will not have the peace and joy that you deserve and want.

4. After you have written down all that you can forgive yourself for, position yourself in front of a mirror, with your large pad of lineless paper at your side along with a pen. Then, taking one statement at a time, look at yourself in the mirror directly in the eyes and say your name. Then say, "I forgive you for…" and fill in the rest of the sentence with whatever it is that you are forgiving yourself for.

5. In response to the reading of any of the above statements, if any feelings surface, either say them out loud, shout them, or even better, write them down on your large pad of paper.

6. Let them all out. Remember that any resistance, anger, or anything else you could be feeling, is residue from past beliefs trying to leave you through being pushed out by The Divine White Light trying to create greater space for itself in your life. Just let the feeling out, scream, talk, mouth, write them out, whatever. Just let them out. For behind them lies the forgiveness we all seek and behind that lies the peace we all deserve.

7. Once you are done with your first forgiving statement, move to the next one, then the next one, then the next one after that, and so on, working your way through each one until you are at the end of your list, no matter how many sessions it takes over however many days.

Once done, move to the next chapter.

Chapter Twelve

What You Really Want With Your Life

Until the dark colored glasses are removed from your life, which is what has just transpired, it is impossible to see who you really are and what you want and are meant to do with your life.

Time to get those questions answered right now.

1. Get out your pens, paper, and whatever device you use to play my CD.

2. Create a time and place for yourself to perform the following exercise.

3. When you are in that space and time, turn

on the first track of the CD and follow the instructions recorded on it.

4. Then as the CD morphs onto the second track, answer the following question, remembering to keep within the lines of the instructions you have already been given on how to approach your writing in this book.

What is it that I really want in my life?

Be very specific and make sure to approach the answering of this question from all angles including the mental, physical, spiritual, emotional, personal, romantic, vocational, and any other perspectives possible, remembering to let the writing lead you and not vice versa.

Chapter Thirteen

What Do I Have To Do To...?

NOW THAT YOU REALLY KNOW WHAT YOUR SOUL IS calling you to have in your life, let's find out what plans it has for acquiring them.

1. Have the necessary tools handy and time reserved to complete this exercise.

2. Once you have moved through the first track of the CD and onto the second, ask yourself the following question in regard to every element you listed in the previous chapter. Address each one of these topics individually, one at a time.

To have the presence of ___ in my life, what do I need to do now, on a routine basis and how often, and in a week, month, year and beyond?

If you previously listed several things that you wanted in your life, you may need to approach each of these individually with this exercise. Either way, don't move on to the next chapter until you have run through each of your wants through the above question.

Chapter Fourteen

Fish, Animal, or Fowl

THERE ARE TWO STAGES TO MAKING ANY SIGNIFICANT alteration in your life.

The first stage involves uprooting your old beliefs and limitations, which have been responsible for creating the life that you had. Some of you may choose to keep moving forward while some may not.

The second stage involves creating the life, in this case your Write Life, which you have felt called to do.

Of course, up until this time, the majority of the life you had was dependent upon what you thought you needed, or needed to avoid, in response to your fears.

That has all changed now through previous exercises, and the room has been prepared for the complete insertion of TUF's White Light into your life.

Possibly for the first time in your life, you are now seeing yourself as TUF sees you. Before going any further, let's look at what that looks like.

As TUF Sees You

1. Move through the first track of the CD and into the second.

2. Once there, respond to the following questions a second time, paying special attention to the "why" segments as you do so. As with the other exercises you have already done, the completion of this one may take several sessions strung over several days.

If I were a road, where would I lead, and why?

If I were a fish, animal or fowl, what would I be, and why?

What one situation or event, more than any other in my life, has done more to make me who I am; and why and how has it done so?

Who has wronged you, hurt you?
What was it that was done?
When did it transpire and how has that adversely affected you in the direction and the quality of your life?

What is it that I really want in my life?

If you would sketch them out, or cut photos out of magazines and paste them on a large piece of lineless paper, what would they look like? Take time to flush all of them out now on a large, lineless piece of paper.

Chapter Fifteen

Your Game Plan

OKAY, IT'S GREAT THAT YOU HAVE CLEARED OUT all that has stood in the way of your release and you can now live through who you really are. It's also great that you now know what you want and what you have to do to get it. But there is still one essential missing ingredient for all your aspirations to come true. The one thing that is missing is a game plan.

Winston Churchill said it best when he confirmed, "He who fails to plan is planning to fail."

1. Have near you the materials which have become so familiar to you by now. Make sure you have established the space you need to perform this final exercise, then turn on your CD, which will move through Track One and onto the second. Once Track Two starts playing, do what is

referred to as a circle drawing around the words, "My game plan for succeeding with every aspect of my life. "What is a circle drawing? Simply put, this technique, which was created by Gabriele Rico and which forms the cornerstone of her book *Writing the Natural Way*, is a brainstorming technique liberally applying the use of circles around each and every expression that comes out of you. Why circles? Because they are non-linear. They have no beginning and no end. Thus, the use of them will confuse your logical mind, which simply will not know what to do with them. As a result, it will transfer whatever you write in them over to your right brain, which will utilize the information inside the circles as a catalyst and will begin dialoguing back to you as a result. Once you have made that shift, you have also made your shift into communication with TUF.

2. Remember to liberally employ the use of the circle surrounding each and every one of the expressions that fire out of you while brainstorming as fast as you can. Let the writing, as you have grown used to doing, lead the way. Also keep in mind that as you begin this circle drawing exercise, which will lead you to create a spider web of expressions on the page in front of you, your thoughts and feelings will initially come out in a very abrupt staccato fashion

but quickly you will open up to the writing of phrases and sentences.

3. Once you begin writing longer phrases and/or sentences, leave the use of the circles behind, transfer your efforts to another lineless piece of paper and begin writing on a linear basis for as long as you need, until every thing and every aspect you have to share about your game plan(s) has been covered.

Chapter Sixteen

Your Contract

N O CLAIMS; NO GAME PLAN IS GUARANTEED TO BE accomplished unless it is reduced to some sort of contractual form. So…

1. Get all you need handy, enter into a quiet space and turn on Track One of the CD. Once it moves into Track Two, do a circle drawing around the following words: "My formal contract to do as my soul is leading me to do translates into the following actions, sequences, and time frames." Use the same exact approach with this circle drawing as was shared with you in the previous chapter, including the movement into writing in a linear fashion. Then boil down everything you had to

say into an actual contract, dated and signed.

2. Once you have completed the writing of your contract, type it up, sign it and send it to everyone in your life who would most benefit from seeing it; especially those supposed adversaries who would do their darndest, oftentimes through intimidation or criticism, to antagonize you into living it.

3. Once you have completed this step, turn the page, finish the book, and live, really live your life.

Chapter Seventeen

Where Do You Go from Here?

THE ANSWER TO THE QUESTION THAT SERVES AS THE title of this chapter is easy: anywhere you want.

With the direct power, grace, speed and love of TUF behind you, anything is possible—anything!

So what are you waiting for?

Take the necessary steps to live that life, the one you always dreamed of.

If you need further guidance along the way, you know how to get it. Just use your own questions to ask TUF what you need to know.

If you run into a block or a jam in your life and you're not sure how to get out of it, so stuck that you can't even come up with your own queries, reuse some of the ones from this book. They will be sure to release you again.

Has this path led you to want to write or publish a book?

I certainly can help there. I would be honored to help you as I have several options available for doing so from my books, webinars, CDs, totally unique interactive computer programs, and retreats.

Check me out further if you are interested.

Either way, I sincerely hope that it is not long before the paths of our lives cross again…

Tom

Made in the USA
San Bernardino, CA
20 July 2016